AN AUGMENTED REALITY
SCIENCE EXPERIENCE

CURIOUS PEARL

SCIENCE GIRL

CURIOUS PEARL EXPLAINS STATES OF MATTER

by Eric Braun

illustrated by Stephanie Dehennin

PICTURE WINDOW BOOKS

a capstone imprint

Curious Pearl here! Do you like science? I sure do! I have all sorts of fun tools to help me observe and investigate, but my favorite tool is my science notebook. That's where I write down questions and facts that help me learn more about science. Would you like to join me on my science adventures? You're in for a special surprise!

Download the Capstone 4D app!

Videos for all of the sidebars in this book are at your fingertips with the 4D app.

To download the Capstone 4D app:

- Search in the Apple App Store or Google Play for "Capstone 4D"
- Click Install (Android) or Get, then Install (Apple)
- Open the application
- Scan any page with this icon

You can also access the additional resources on the web at www.capstone4D.com using the password **pearl.matter**

CURIOUS PEARL
SCIENCE GIRL

Isn't summer the best? There is lots of time for playing and riding my bike. I get to hang out with my little brother, Peter, too.

Peter likes summer as much as I do. And Peter loves ice pops. He loves them like the sky loves the stars. Like I love science!

Today Peter and I were playing outside with our friends. Suddenly, Peter screamed, "We need ice pops!"

"That sounds serious!" I told my friends. "I better find some ice pops."

I went inside to find an ice pop. But we didn't have any. I grabbed cheese and crackers. I got apples and peanut butter.

"Ice pops! Ice pops!" he cried.

"All right," I said. "Let's make some ice pops out of juice."

"We can't turn juice into an ice pop!" Peter said.

"Sure we can," I said. "It's just a matter of MATTER."

"What is the matter?" he asked.

"Nothing is the matter," I said. "But everything is MATTER. Juice, ice pops, air, chairs, and even people are made of matter."

"Wait," Peter said. "Air? Air isn't made of anything."

"Yes, even air! It's a gas. Gas is one state of matter. Liquid is another state — like this orange juice. The other state is solid. This counter is a solid." I knocked my knuckles on it. "And so are ice pops."

Peter shook his head. "I still don't get how air is matter," he said.

I was about to explain it to him. But then I realized I didn't really get it either.

"Let's see what we can observe about these states of matter," I said.

"Well, if air is matter, it doesn't have any shape," Peter said.

"Eureka! That's true!" I said. Eureka is a scientific word. I use it when I make a new discovery.

I pulled out my trusty science notebook and pencil.

Gas, like air, has no shape. You can move through it.

"Compare that to liquid," I said.

"Liquid just sort of sloshes and changes shape," Peter said. "If we poured it on the floor, it would be flat like the floor too."

"Please don't pour it on the floor," I said. You never know what little brothers will do!

"The orange juice in the ice pop mold is shaped like the mold," I noted.

Peter stuck his finger into one of the molds.

"And you can poke your finger into it," he said.

I wrote about liquids in my science notebook.

Liquid changes shape to fit its container. Like air, things can move through liquid.

"Are the ice pops ready to go in the freezer yet?"
Peter asked.

"Yes," I said. "But first, tell me what you observe
about solids."

"Solids are solid!" he said, grinning.

"Eureka! That's true!" I said. "But what does *that*
mean?"

Peter patted the counter, testing it. He tapped his foot on the floor — another solid. He picked up the ice pop molds and felt them.

"I think solid means it has its own shape, and you can't change it," he said.

"Good thinking!" I replied.

I was about to make a note in my notebook. But just then, Peter dropped the ice pop molds. Orange juice splattered all over! And guess what else? One of the molds broke in half.

"So you *can* change a solid's shape," I said.

Solids do not change shape to fit a container. But you can break, carve, or sculpt them to change their shape.

You can't move through a solid.

I helped Peter clean up the mess. Then we poured orange juice into another set of ice pop molds. We put the molds into the freezer.

"They will take some time to freeze," I told Peter. "Let's eat lunch while we wait." I took out a box of cheesy macaroni. Next, I poured water into a pot. Then I found Mom to help me turn on the stove.

Peter said, "One time, I lost an ice pop in bed."

"Yuck!" I replied.

"Yeah," he said. "When I found it again, it had melted. So a solid can become a liquid. But when does that happen, exactly?"

"Eureka! Good observation!" I said. "Liquids freeze at a freezing point. When water freezes, it becomes a solid — ice. Water's freezing point is 32 degrees Fahrenheit (0 degrees Celsius). That's also its melting point. So if the temperature of ice goes above 32 degrees F (0 degrees C), it will turn into a liquid."

"What about gas?" Peter asked. "Can anything turn into a gas?"

"Look!" I said. I pointed to the water boiling on the stove. Steam was rising from the pot. "Liquid turns into a gas at its boiling point. Water's boiling point is 212 degrees F (100 degrees C)."

Time for another note in my science notebook!

Matter changes state when its temperature changes enough.

"Even the ice pop molds would become a liquid if they got hot enough," I said.

"But I still don't get how air is supposed to be matter," Peter said. "It's like nothing."

After lunch, Peter and I searched online. We learned about atoms. All matter is made up of atoms. The state of any matter changes, depending on how close together the atoms are.

"Huh?" Peter said.

"I'll show you," I said.

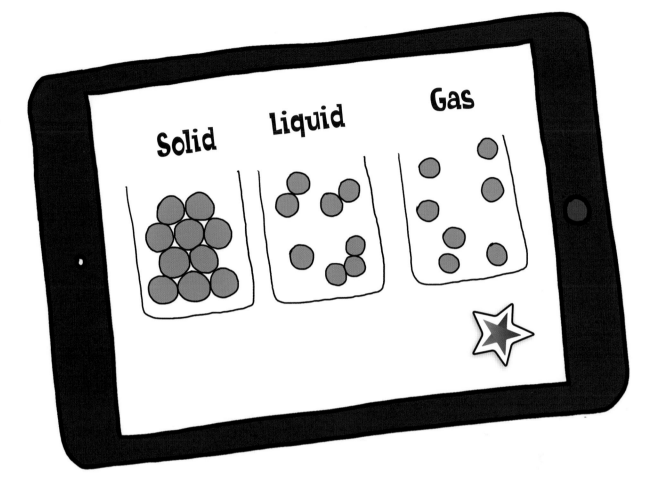

I explained the drawings to Peter. "Atoms in a solid are very close together. They can't move, and you can't get through them. In a liquid, the atoms are farther apart. They can move a little bit. The atoms in a gas are even farther apart. It's easy to pass through a gas like air or steam."

"Pearl?" Peter asked.

"Yes?" I said. I tried to imagine the next science question he might ask. I was ready to answer it!

"Are the ice pops ready?" he asked.

Well, that's an easy question to answer. I opened the freezer and checked. They were done! Peter and I brought ice pops to our friends outside.

"You know," Peter said, licking his lips. "I like science!"

SCIENCE ACTIVITY

If you like frozen treats, you can make ice pops like Pearl and Peter did. Or you can get a bit more interesting and make ice cream! This is a fun way to see liquid change into a solid.

What you need:

1 cup half-and-half

¼ cup white sugar

½ teaspoon vanilla extract

½ cup table salt or rock salt

2 cups ice cubes

1 sandwich-size zip baggie

1 gallon-size zip baggie

What You Do:

1. Pour the half-and-half, sugar, and vanilla into the small zip baggie. Zip it up tight so it doesn't leak!

2. Put the ice cubes and salt into the gallon baggie.

3. Put the smaller baggie inside the bigger baggie along with the ice and salt. Seal the baggie.

4. Hold the baggie by the zipper at the top, and shake it. Keep shaking it until the ingredients in the small baggie are solid. This will take about 10 minutes.

5. Remove the smaller baggie from the bigger one, and serve your ice cream!

If you like, you can add your extra treats into the mixture before you shake the ice cream. But doing that will make the ice cream take longer to freeze. You can also put your extras on top after serving.

GLOSSARY

freeze—to become a solid or icy at a very low temperature

gas—a form of matter that is not solid or liquid; it can move about freely and does not have a definite shape

liquid—a form of matter that is wet and can be poured and takes the shape if its container

matter—anything that has weight and takes up space, such as a gas, a liquid, or a solid

melt—to change from a solid to a liquid; ice or snow melts above 32 degrees Fahrenheit (0 degrees Celsius)

observe—to watch someone or something closely in order to learn something

particle—an extremely tiny piece of matter; particles are too small to be seen with the naked eye

solid—a form of matter that does not easily change shape and can't be passed through

READ MORE

Braun, Eric. *Joe-Joe the Wizard Brews Up Solids, Liquids, and Gases.* In the Science Lab. Mankato, Minn.: Picture Window Books, 2012.

Zoehfeld, Kathleen Weidner. *What Is the World Made Of?: All About Solids, Liquids, and Gases.* New York: Harper Collins, 2015.

INTERNET SITES

Use FactHound to find Internet sites related to this book.

Visit *www.facthound.com*

Just type in 9781515813422 and go.

CRITICAL THINKING QUESTIONS

When have you seen matter change states? Name as many examples as you can.

Have you ever seen dew on grass or plants in the morning? Where do you think it comes from?

Can you think of a way to get the salt out of salt water? Explain your idea.

MORE BOOKS IN THE SERIES

INDEX

Thanks to our adviser for his expertise, research, and advice:
Christopher T. Ruhland, PhD
Professor of Biological Sciences
Department of Biology
Minnesota State University, Mankato

Editor: Shelly Lyons
Designer: Ted Williams
Art Director: Nathan Gassman
Production Specialist: Katy LaVigne
The illustrations in this book were digitally produced.

Picture Window Books are published by Capstone, 1710 Roe Crest Drive, North Mankato, Minnesota 56003
www.mycapstone.com

Library of Congress Cataloging-in-Publication Data
Cataloging-in-Publication information is on file with Library of Congress.
Names: Braun, Eric, author. | Dehennin, Stephanie, illustrator.
Title: Curious Pearl Explains States of Matter: 4D An Augmented Reality Science Experience
ISBN 978-1-5158-1342-2 (library binding)
ISBN 978-1-5158-1346-0 (paperback)
ISBN 978-1-5158-1358-3 (eBook PDF)

Printed and bound in the USA.
022020   003243